39 AMAZING EXPERIMENTS WITH THE MEGA-MAGNET

By Brian Rohrig

Illustrated by Michele Murphy

TEACHER'S
Discovery
©2009 American Eagle Co., Inc.

All experiments in this book are to be performed only under competent adult supervision. Neither the author nor the publisher assume any liability whatsoever for any damage caused or injury sustained while performing the experiments contained in this book.

Teachers Discovery
2741 Paldan Drive
Auburn Hills, MI 48326

For Natalie

Other books by Brian Rohrig:

150 Captivating Chemistry Experiments Using Household Substances

150 More Captivating Chemistry Experiments Using Household Substances

101 Intriguing Labs, Projects, and Activities for the Chemistry Classroom

39 Dazzling Experiments with Dry Ice

39 Fantastic Experiments with the Fizz-Keeper

39 Spectacular Experiments with Soda Pop

ACKNOWLEDGEMENTS

Thanks to Frank Reuter for carefully and thoroughly editing this text. Any and all errors are strictly my own.

Illustrations by Michele Murphy

Printed in Roseville, Mich.

Cover design by Kristi Gerner

TABLE OF CONTENTS

Introduction 8
Safety Precautions 10

1. What Is Attracted To The
   Mega-Magnet? 11
2. Are Nickels Really Made of Nickel? 14
3. A Magnetic Penny Pyramid 17
4. Mapping A Magnetic Field 21
5. Testing The Mega-Magnet's Strength 24
6. Testing The Mega-Magnet's Strength:
   Part 2 28
7. Magnetic Shielding 32
8. A Trick To Impress Your Friends 36
9. Underwater Magnetism 39
10. Making A Silverware Sculpture 41
11. Detecting Counterfeit Bills 44
12. Does Your Cereal Contain Iron? 46
13. Erasing A Cassette Tape 49
14. Magnetic Floppy Disks 52
15. Is Your Soil Magnetic? 55
16. Distortion Of A TV Image 58
17. Deflection Of Electrons By A Magnetic
    Field 60
18. How Does A Compass Work? 63
19. Make Your Own Magnet 67
20. Suspending A Paper Clip 69
21. Make Your Own Compass 72
22. Eerie Effects 75
23. Killing Time 77

24. Finding The Poles Of The
    Mega-Magnet **79**
25. Repulsion Of Like Poles **82**
26. Do Electric Currents Produce Magnetic
    Fields? **85**
27. Demonstration Of Eddy Currents **88**
28. Demonstration Of Eddy Currents:
    Part 2 .... **92**
29. Is Water Magnetic? **95**
30. Is Water Magnetic? Part 2 .... **98**
31. Are Iron Tablets Attracted To A
    Magnet? **100**
32. Paramagnetism of Oxygen **103**
33. Magnetizing A Hammer **104**
34. Observation Of The Curie Point **110**
35. A Magnetic Marble Game **114**
36. Stud Finder **117**
37. A Magnetic Pendulum **119**
38. Magnetic Paint **123**
39. Storing Your Mega-Magnet **126**

Learn More About Magnets **128**
Bibliography **129**

INTRODUCTION

Congratulations on your purchase of a Mega-Magnet! As one of the world's most powerful permanent magnets, it is sure to provide many hours of fun and scientific inquiry. The Mega-Magnet is manufactured from neodymium, a rare earth metal. The Mega-Magnet also contains iron and boron. Since neodymium (atomic number 60 on the Periodic Table) is a rare earth metal, the Mega-Magnet is often referred to as a rare-earth magnet. The first commercial rare-earth magnets, introduced in 1970, were made from cobalt and samarium, expensive elements which limited production. In 1983, the less expensive neodymium-iron-boron magnet was developed.

Since a rare-earth magnet can do what an ordinary magnet 50 times larger can do, the development of these supermagnets made it possible to miniaturize much of our electronic technology. Rare-earth magnets are commonly found in motors, computers, stereo speakers, and the compact earphones used with a Walkman. Furthermore, these neodymium magnets are so powerful that a device called a "Gripper" has been developed, which, when attached to a person's feet and hands, enables the user to scale metal bridges, towers, or steel buildings.

39 Amazing Experiments with the Mega-Magnet

The Mega-Magnet that comes with this book is a surplus magnet that has been salvaged from old computer disk drives. Very strong permanent magnets tend to be brittle, so it is not unusual for small pieces to chip off during use. Your Mega-Magnet may be slightly nicked or chipped, but this will in no way interfere with its quality or magnetic force. Surplus magnets have been used to keep the price affordable. This same magnet purchased new would be quite expensive.

Before doing anything with your Mega-Magnet, be sure to study and observe the safety precautions which follow. The failure to use and store the magnet properly could cause serious problems.

39 Amazing Experiments with the Mega-Magnet

SAFETY PRECAUTIONS

It is very important that the following safety precautions be observed when using the Mega-Magnet:

1. Keep the Mega-Magnet away from all electronic devices, such as pacemakers, television sets, computers, and stereos.
2. Keep the Mega-Magnet away from all media that store information magnetically: credit cards, bankcards, floppy disks, cassette tapes, videotapes, and magnetic hotel room keys.
3. Be careful not to pinch your fingers between the magnet and a metallic surface.
4. Under no circumstances should two Mega-Magnets be brought together! They can severely pinch your fingers. They also may shatter, and will be very difficult to separate.
5. We advise that you wrap the Mega-Magnet with electrical tape—available at any hardware store—to prevent chipping and damage to surfaces.
6. Keep the Mega-Magnet out of the reach of small children.
7. The Mega-Magnet is only to be used under adult supervision.

39 Amazing Experiments with the Mega-Magnet

Experiment # 1:
WHAT IS ATTRACTED TO THE MEGA-MAGNET?

Objective: To determine the type of objects that are attracted to the Mega-Magnet.

Materials:
- Miscellaneous household objects
- Tin cans from your kitchen cupboard

Safety Precautions:
Only use the Mega-Magnet under adult supervision. Keep the Mega-Magnet away from televisions, computers, software, videotapes, cassette tapes, and credit cards.

Procedure:
1. Using your Mega-Magnet, experiment with as many different household objects as you can find, such as nails, bolts, jewelry, pens, pencils, and tin cans from your kitchen cupboard.
2. Make a list of all objects that are attracted to the Mega-Magnet.
3. Make another list of those objects that are not attracted to the Mega-Magnet.

39 Amazing Experiments with the Mega-Magnet

4. What do the members of each list have in common?

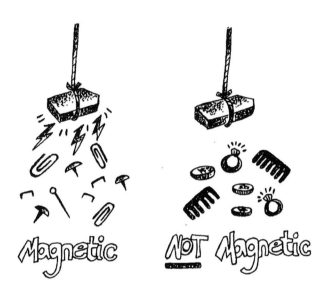

Explanation: You will probably notice that only metallic objects can be picked up with the Mega-Magnet. Non-metallic objects, such as plastic and rubber, are not attracted to a magnet. But among the metals, only substances composed of iron, nickel, or cobalt will be attracted to a magnet at room temperature. These three elements are ferromagnetic, which means they are strongly attracted to a magnet. Probably most of the items that your magnet attracts are composed of iron, or an alloy of iron, such as steel. If a substance is not attracted to a magnet, it is called diamagnetic.

Diamagnetic materials are actually slightly repelled by a magnetic field.

Most tin cans can easily be picked up with the Mega-Magnet. It may seem odd that a tin can is attracted to a magnet, since tin is not ferromagnetic. But most tin cans are actually made of steel, with just a thin coating of tin for corrosion resistance. Steel rusts, but tin does not.

Try picking up a soda can with the Mega-Magnet. It will not be attracted to a magnet, since soda cans are made of aluminum, which is diamagnetic.

39 Amazing Experiments with the Mega-Magnet

Experiment # 2:
ARE NICKELS REALLY MADE OF NICKEL?

Objective: To determine the difference between American and Canadian nickels.

Materials:
- American nickel
- Canadian nickel minted before 1982
- Other Canadian coins
- Variety of foreign coins (available from a coin shop)

Safety Precautions: Only use the Mega-Magnet under adult supervision. Keep the Mega-Magnet away from televisions, computers, software, videotapes, cassette tapes, and credit cards.

Procedure:
1. Test an American nickel with the Mega-Magnet. What happens? Try other American coins as well.
2. Now test a Canadian nickel with the Mega-Magnet? What happens?
3. Try other Canadian coins and other types of foreign coins. Are they attracted to the Mega-Magnet?

39 Amazing Experiments with the Mega-Magnet

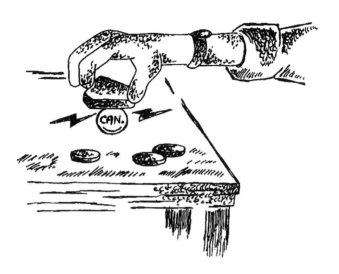

Explanation: Since nickel is ferromagnetic, you would expect a nickel to be attracted to a magnet. But American nickels are not made purely of nickel, but rather an alloy composed of 75% copper and only 25% nickel. Since copper is not attracted to a magnet, neither is the American nickel. From 1942-1945, the composition of the nickel was changed so that nickel could be used for the war effort. The composition of these World War II era nickels are 56% copper, 35% silver, and 9% manganese.

If the Canadian nickel you tested was minted before 1982, it will be attracted to your magnet. Other types of Canadian coins are still magnetic, since they are composed primarily of nickel. It is

39 Amazing Experiments with the Mega-Magnet

somewhat ironic that the only Canadian coin (besides pennies) currently not made of nickel is the nickel! The $2.00 Canadian coin is composed of an outer ring of nickel and an inner ring of brass. The inner ring is not attracted to a magnet, but the outer ring is. Many other foreign coins are magnetic as well. These will either be composed of nickel or steel.

A criminal case was brought against a bus driver for stealing thousands of dollars worth of coins by using a long pole attached to a magnet to remove coins from the coin deposit box on his bus. Where do you think this crime occurred? After thinking about it, check the answer below.

Magnetism is also used to protect the owners of soda machines from fraud. People will occasionally use metal washers or other objects in place of real money to activate a soda machine. In the United States, each deposited coin is tested to see if it is magnetic. If it is, the "coin" is rejected and no soda will be dispensed, since American coins are not magnetic. This explains why Canadian coins cannot be used in soda machines in the U.S. How might soda machines in Canada differ?

[The mystery of the missing coins: The answer is Canada since most of their coins are magnetic.]

Experiment # 3:
A MAGNETIC PENNY PYRAMID

Objective: To discover that a magnet can temporarily magnetize other objects.

Materials:
- Ten 1943 steel pennies (available from a coin shop) or steel washers

Safety Precautions: Only use the Mega-Magnet under adult supervision. Keep the Mega-Magnet away from televisions, computers, software, videotapes, cassette tapes, and credit cards.

Procedure:
1. Place one 1943 penny on edge on the top face of the Mega-Magnet. Hold onto this penny while constructing the rest of the pyramid.
2. On top of this penny, place 2 more pennies on edge.
3. Construct two more layers, of three and four pennies each, until you end up with an inverted pyramid.
4. Now turn the magnet over so the single penny and the entire pyramid are beneath

39 Amazing Experiments with the Mega-Magnet

the magnet. With a little practice, you will be able to remove your finger and allow the pyramid to remain intact.

5. Finally, grasp the single penny (now the top of your inverted pyramid) and carefully remove it from the magnet a few millimeters. With a little practice, the entire pyramid will remain intact even though no part of it is touching the magnet!

Explanation: This experiment could also be performed with British pennies, which are currently made from steel. The 1943 steel penny is the only American coin that is attracted to a magnet. During World War II copper was needed for the war effort, so in 1943 all U.S. minted pennies were made from steel. Steel, being an alloy of iron, is attracted to a magnet. You can buy these steel pennies from any coin shop for about $.50 each.

The magnetic field of the Mega-Magnet is strong enough to hold the pyramid in place without touching any of the pennies. Each penny that is near the Mega-Magnet temporarily becomes a magnet itself. These temporary magnets cause other pennies that are touching them to become magnetized as well. As a result, each penny in the pyramid becomes a magnet. But if the Mega-Magnet is removed the pennies immediately become unmagnetized and tumble into a pile.

In a permanent magnet, groups of atoms known as domains all point in the same direction. Each domain is itself a tiny magnet, with a north and a south pole. A domain can be as large as 1 mm in length and width. Within every atom in a domain electrons spin in the same direction. Many, many electrons spinning in the same direction within a domain gives rise to an observable magnetic field. This magnetic field can cause domains within neighboring atoms to temporarily become aligned and become magnets themselves. In this experiment, each penny temporarily becomes a magnet, which can in turn induce a magnetic field in other pennies surrounding it, causing them to become magnets.

If you examine the electron configuration of the three ferromagnetic elements – iron, cobalt, and nickel – you will notice that they have unpaired electrons in their d orbitals that spin in the same direction. (An orbital is a region of space within an atom where you have the greatest probability of finding electrons.) Each of these unpaired electrons spin in the same direction. Many electrons spinning in the same direction will give rise to a magnetic field where its effect can be readily observed. A diamagnetic element, on the other hand, will have no unpaired electrons in their orbitals. Since each orbital within an atom can only hold 2 electrons, each of these electrons will spin in the opposite direction, thus canceling out each other's magnetic field. Examples of diamagnetic elements are copper, gold, silver, and lead. Diamagnetic elements are slightly repelled by a magnetic field.

Experiment # 4:
MAPPING A MAGNETIC FIELD

Objective: To discover the effect of the Mega-Magnet's magnetic field.

Materials:

- White piece of cardboard
- Iron filings (Available from a science teacher or a metal shop. Make your own by filing down an iron nail or breaking up a piece of steel wool.)
- 20 oz plastic soda bottle

Safety Precautions: Only use the Mega-Magnet under adult supervision. Keep the Mega-Magnet away from televisions, computers, software, videotapes, cassette tapes, and credit cards.

Procedure:

1. Sprinkle a liberal amount of iron filings on a piece of white cardboard.
2. Place the Mega-Magnet underneath the cardboard. Observe the pattern that forms.
3. Place some iron filings in a 20 oz soda bottle, cap the bottle, and place it on its side. Place the Mega-Magnet on the

39 Amazing Experiments with the Mega-Magnet

outside of the bottle and observe the pattern that forms.

Explanation: A magnetic field surrounds every magnet. This is an invisible region where the attractive pull of the magnet is experienced by any ferromagnetic object that enters this field. Magnetic field lines flow outward from the magnet's north pole and then around the magnet to its south pole. The magnetic field is strongest at the poles where the magnetic lines of force are the closest together. The magnetic field becomes weaker as the distance from the poles increases.

The pattern of your filings is a good way to determine the location of the poles of your magnet. At the same time it demonstrates the magnetic field surrounding the Mega-Magnet. However, since the poles of the Mega-Magnet are on opposite faces of the magnet, the full extent of the magnetic field can best be demonstrated by submerging the entire magnet in iron filings. This is not recommended, however, since it will be very difficult to remove the filings from the powerful magnet!

39 Amazing Experiments with the Mega-Magnet

Experiment # 5:
TESTING THE MEGA-MAGNET'S STRENGTH

Objective: To determine how much weight the Mega-Magnet is capable of lifting.

Materials:
- Various household objects: nails, paper clips, thumbtacks, etc.
- Kitchen scale or digital balance

Safety Precautions: Only use the Mega-Magnet under adult supervision. Keep the Mega-Magnet away from televisions, computers, software, videotapes, cassette tapes, and credit cards.

Procedure:
1. Use your Mega-Magnet to pick up as many objects as possible, such as nails, paper clips, etc.
2. Once your magnet has approached its limit as to how much it can hold, remove all of the objects and weigh them on the scale. The total may surprise you!

Explanation: The most enjoyable thing about any magnet is its ability to pick up things. You will be amazed at the strength of the Mega-Magnet. It seems like its strength is unlimited. However, it can't pick up a car, at least not a passenger vehicle!

The strength of the magnetic field produced by a magnet is measured by the metric unit known as the gauss (G). This unit is named after the German mathematician Karl Friedric Gauss (1777-1855), who made many important contributions to the theory of magnetism. The Mega-Magnet has a magnetic field strength of approximately

39 Amazing Experiments with the Mega-Magnet

12,300 G. A refrigerator magnet has a magnetic field strength of only about 10 G. A typical household magnet will generally not have a magnetic field strength greater than 1,000 or 2,000 G. Electromagnets have produced continuous magnetic fields that have exceeded 200,000 G! The greatest magnetic fields in the universe are believed to be within neutron stars, where the magnetic field strength is a trillion G. By contrast, the magnetic field strength of the Earth is about .5 G. So your Mega-Magnet is about 1000 times more powerful than a refrigerator magnet, and 20,000 times more powerful than the magnetic field of the Earth!

39 Amazing Experiments with the Mega-Magnet

The strength of a magnetic field is determined by the number of magnetic lines of force that flow from the north to the south pole of the magnet. The more magnetic field lines, the stronger the magnetic field. The number of magnetic lines of force per square centimeter of area is a measure of the strength of the magnetic field. 1 G is equal to 1 magnetic field line per square centimeter. The magnetic field surrounding your Mega-Magnet therefore contains 12,300 magnetic field lines per square centimeter!

39 Amazing Experiments with the Mega-Magnet

Experiment # 6:
TESTING THE MEGA-MAGNET'S STRENGTH: PART 2

Objective: To test the strength of the Mega-Magnet.

Materials:
- Paper clips
- Ordinary household magnet
- Several decks of cards

Safety Precautions: Only use the Mega-Magnet under adult supervision. Keep the Mega-Magnet away from televisions, computers, software, videotapes, cassette tapes, and credit cards.

Procedure:
1. Attach a single paper clip to the Mega-Magnet and allow it to dangle.
2. Attach more paper clips to this one, until you have formed a chain that can support the maximum number of paper clips. How many paper clips can the Mega-Magnet support?

39 Amazing Experiments with the Mega-Magnet

3. Repeat this procedure with an ordinary household magnet. How much more powerful is the Mega-Magnet?
4. Now place the Mega-Magnet on top of a deck of cards.
5. Hold the deck away from you, and place a paper clip underneath the deck of cards. What happens?
6. Continue adding cards from a second deck to the card pile until the Mega-Magnet can no longer attract the paper clip through the cards.
7. Experiment with other substances, such as plastic, wood, and metal. What types of material does the Mega-Magnet most effectively penetrate?

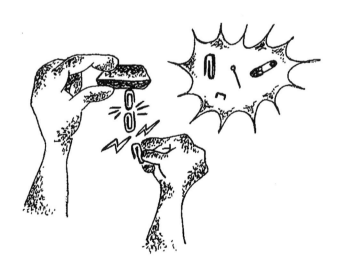

39 Amazing Experiments with the Mega-Magnet

Explanation: The Mega-Magnet is strong enough to temporarily induce a magnetic field in the paper clips that are attached to it. These paper clips in turn induce a temporary magnetic field in the paper clips that are attached to them. The same thing can be attempted with pins, needles, staples, etc. The lighter the object, the longer the chain you will be able to form. A much longer chain can be achieved with the Mega-Magnet than with an ordinary household magnet.

The magnetic field surrounding the Mega-Magnet decreases with increasing distance. Placing materials between the magnet and the paper clip will serve to weaken the attraction between the objects. But it is still surprising to see how many cards the magnetic field of the

Mega-Magnet can effectively penetrate. This same experiment can also be repeated with books or magazines.

An interesting variation on the above experiment can be performed using a deck of ferromagnetic playing cards, which themselves are attracted to a magnet. These are available from Kling Magnetics, Inc., at www.kling.com or 518-392-4000. Do you think the Mega-Magnet can attract more or less paper clips through this deck of cards than through a deck of ordinary playing cards? There is only one way to find out!

Experiment # 7:
MAGNETIC SHIELDING

Objective: To determine which substances are most effective at shielding the Mega-Magnet.

Materials:
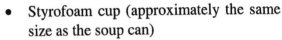
- Empty metal soup can (with the top removed)
- Plastic cup (approximately the same size as the soup can)
- Styrofoam cup (approximately the same size as the soup can)
- Paper clips

Safety Precautions: Only use the Mega-Magnet under adult supervision. Keep the Mega-Magnet away from televisions, computers, software, videotapes, cassette tapes, and credit cards.

Procedure:
1. Invert a soup can and place the Mega-Magnet on the bottom of the can, which will now be facing upward. Attempt to dangle a paper clip from the inside wall of the open end of the can.
2. Repeat with the plastic cup and then with the Styrofoam cup. Are you successful?

39 Amazing Experiments with the Mega-Magnet

Explanation: You should be able to dangle a paper clip from the wall of the open end of the soup can. If not, attempt to place the paper clip higher up on the side of the can. You will not be able to dangle a paper clip from the bottom of either the plastic or the Styrofoam cups. At first glance, it may appear that plastic and Styrofoam are better magnetic insulators than the can. This is certainly true as far as insulating from an electric current, but an electrical insulator does little to stop a magnetic field. Magnetic field lines can easily penetrate even the best electrical insulator.

However, like an electrical field, magnetic fields will tend to take the path of least resistance. Since the magnetic field lines can more easily line up in a ferromagnetic material, they can easily penetrate the iron can. The magnetic field lines travel through the sides of the can, which explains why the paper clip is attracted to it. As a result, the area in the middle of the can is not affected as much by the magnetic field. By using a ferromagnetic material, you can easily "trick" the magnetic field lines to flow around an object that you want to keep insulated.

A similar principle works with lightning. The safest place to be during an electrical storm is in a metal building, as long as the floor is not made of metal and you do not touch the sides. If lightning strikes the building, the metal walls carry the current through the walls and into the ground, effectively shielding objects within the building from the lightning strike. For the same reason, a car is a relatively safe place to be during an electrical storm. Like magnetism, electricity will take the path of least resistance.

A material that is not ferromagnetic will do little to stop the penetration of a magnetic field. But you can still insulate from a magnetic field by using nonferromagnetic material. For example, wrapping the Mega-Magnet in many layers of bubble wrap would prevent it from picking up even a paper clip, but this is only because we have greatly increased the distance from the magnet to the paper clip. The stronger the magnetic field, however, the greater the distance it can travel.

It is often necessary to provide protection from a powerful magnetic field. Some stereo speakers contain very powerful magnets, which can distort the image on your television screen if the speakers are placed too close to it. If the magnets within the speakers were better insulated, this would not happen.

When powerful magnets are shipped, it is necessary to shield the magnetic field. This is often done by placing sheets of steel around the magnets within the package, redirecting the magnetic field. This is especially important if magnets are to be shipped on an airplane. A powerful magnetic field can disrupt an airplane's sensitive instruments. One way to test whether or not a package containing magnets has been effectively shielded is to dangle a paper clip on a string along all sides of the box. If the paper clip experiences no attraction, then the magnetic field has been effectively shielded.

The Mega-Magnet itself is salvaged from old computer disk drives. In order to prevent damage to magnetically recorded information within the computer, the Mega-Magnet must be effectively shielded.

39 Amazing Experiments with the Mega-Magnet

Experiment # 8:
A TRICK TO IMPRESS YOUR FRIENDS

Objective: To demonstrate the strength of the Mega-Magnet.

Materials:
- Paper clips

Safety Precautions: Only use the Mega-Magnet under adult supervision. Keep the Mega-Magnet away from televisions, computers, software, videotapes, cassette tapes, and credit cards.

Procedure:
1. Place the Mega-Magnet on top of your hand and place a paper clip underneath your hand. The paper clip will not fall!
2. Try to dangle another paper clip from the first one. How many paper clips can be supported through your hand by the Mega-Magnet?

Explanation: The Mega-Magnet has tremendous penetrating power, as demonstrated by the above experiment. Its magnetic lines of force can easily penetrate the human hand.

39 Amazing Experiments with the Mega-Magnet

Experiment to see what other body parts the Mega-Magnet is capable of penetrating.

Some people are convinced that placing magnets on their body can make them feel better. A visit to any drugstore will reveal a wide array of magnetic bracelets, patches, and insoles, each with alleged healing properties. Magnets have been sold as cures for arthritis, baldness, asthma, headaches, gout, varicose veins, insomnia, stress, and even cancer.

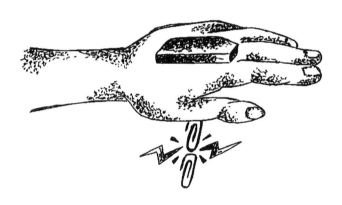

The healing powers of magnets were first touted during the Middle Ages, and were very popular during the first part of the 20th century. During the 1990s, there was a resurgence of interest in the healing power of magnets. This was partly due to the testimonies of some Major League baseball players who were convinced that

39 Amazing Experiments with the Mega-Magnet

wearing magnets increased their speed and stamina.

There is no scientific evidence to support these claims, however. But there is plenty of anecdotal evidence. Anecdotal evidence is based upon personal testimony as opposed to controlled scientific testing. The placebo effect can play a big role. If a person is convinced that a magnet will make him feel better, then the magnet will appear to have the desired effect.

Experiment # 9:
UNDERWATER MAGNETISM

Objective: To determine if a magnet will work underwater.

Materials:

- Glass of water
- Paper clips

Safety Precautions: Only use the Mega-Magnet under adult supervision. Keep the Mega-Magnet away from televisions, computers, software, videotapes, cassette tapes, and credit cards.

Procedure:

1. Fill a glass with water and drop in a paper clip.
2. Attempt to retrieve the paper clip with the Mega-Magnet by inserting the Mega-Magnet in the glass of water. At what point does the paper clip jump up to meet the magnet?
3. Now empty the glass of water and retrieve the paper clip with the magnet. At what point does the paper clip now jump up to meet the magnet? Is there a difference?

39 Amazing Experiments with the Mega-Magnet

Explanation: Water has little effect on the ability of the Mega-Magnet to attract objects to itself. Magnets work just fine underwater. Magnetic fields are capable of penetrating a wide variety of objects. Air, water, and even a vacuum can all be successfully penetrated by a magnetic field.

During World War II, Germany developed magnetic detonation mines that were placed on the bottom of a shallow body of water. The triggering mechanism was a small magnet that looked like a compass needle. When an iron ship passed over this mine, it would detonate and blow up the ship. The Allies were thus forced to come up with methods to demagnetize the iron hulls of the ship, a process known as degaussing. These magnetic mines would obviously not have worked if a magnetic field could not travel through water.

Experiment # 10:
MAKING A SILVERWARE SCULPTURE

Objective: To create modern art using the Mega-Magnet.

Materials:

- Silverware
- Other metallic objects that are attracted to a magnet

Safety Precautions: Only use the Mega-Magnet under adult supervision. Keep the Mega-Magnet away from televisions, computers, software, videotapes, cassette tapes, and credit cards.

Procedure:

1. Open up your silverware drawer and remove any knives or other sharp objects. Place these items aside. They will not be part of this experiment.
2. Attempt to attract as many pieces of silverware as possible with the Mega-Magnet.

39 Amazing Experiments with the Mega-Magnet

3. Arrange the objects to form a visually appealing piece of modern art.
4. Repeat with other metallic objects that are attracted to the Mega-Magnet.

Explanation: Many commercially available varieties of magnetic art are available for purchase. But with a little creativity, you can produce all sorts of unique art using only the Mega-Magnet and materials found around the house. Paper clips, bolts, screws, nails, and steel ball bearings make for some interesting art. The creation of the designs is possible because of the Mega-Magnet's ability to magnetize other objects it comes into contact with. This induced magnetism is in turn passed on to other objects. And by the way, is the silverware in your drawer really made of silver? If it was, it would not be sticking to your Mega-Magnet! Silver is not attracted to a magnet, since it is diamagnetic.

Experiment # 11:
DETECTING COUNTERFEIT BILLS

Objective: To determine if a dollar bill is genuine.

Materials:

- Dollar bill
- Paper clip

Safety Precautions: Only use the Mega-Magnet under adult supervision. Keep the Mega-Magnet away from televisions, computers, software, videotapes, cassette tapes, and credit cards.

Procedure:

1. Poke a hole near the end of a dollar bill with a paper clip, and then attach the paper clip to the dollar bill so that it dangles freely on the paper clip.
2. Holding the bill by the paper clip, bring the Mega-Magnet toward the bottom of the bill. What happens?
3. Repeat this experiment with other types of bills. What do you observe?

39 Amazing Experiments with the Mega-Magnet

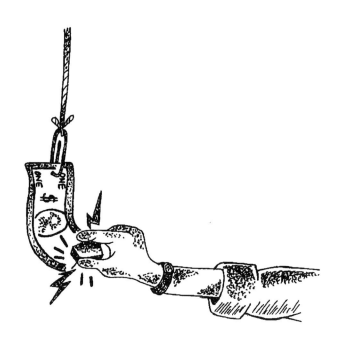

Explanation: Iron is added to the ink in paper currency in order to make it attractive to a magnet. The technique is a counterfeiting prevention measure. This same effect can be observed with other types of paper currency as well. If you have a bill that is not attracted to the Mega-Magnet, you may have a counterfeit on your hands! Test paper currency from other countries. Are these bills attracted to the Mega-Magnet?

39 Amazing Experiments with the Mega-Magnet

Experiment # 12:
DOES YOUR CEREAL CONTAIN IRON?

Objective: To determine what types of cereal contain iron.

Materials:
- Total cereal
- Various other brands of cereal
- Spoon
- Bowl
- White electrical tape

Safety Precautions: Only use the Mega-Magnet under adult supervision. Keep the Mega-Magnet away from televisions, computers, software, videotapes, cassette tapes, and credit cards.

Procedure:
1. Wrap the Mega-Magnet in white electrical tape, so the results of this experiment will be more visible.
2. Place a few Total cereal flakes on the table. Bring your Mega-Magnet very close to them and see what happens. Try sliding the Mega-Magnet ever so gently toward the flakes. If nothing happens, break the

39 Amazing Experiments with the Mega-Magnet

cereal into smaller pieces and then try again.

3. Try floating the flakes on water and then bring the Mega-Magnet near. Observe.

4. Now take a half-bowl of Total cereal and add enough water to cover the flakes. Stir with a spoon until a slurry has formed. Now stir the mixture with the Mega-Magnet, using a regular circular motion. You will get the slurry all over your hands, but it will wash off. After a few minutes, examine the end of the Mega-Magnet. What do you observe?

5. Repeat with other types of cereal. What happens?

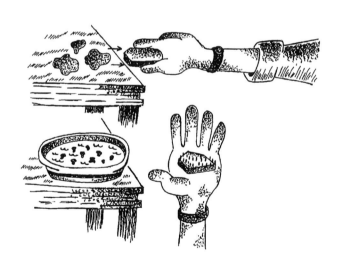

39 Amazing Experiments with the Mega-Magnet

Explanation: Very fine iron filings are added to many cereals that are fortified with iron. This iron is readily attracted to the Mega-Magnet. When water is added to the cereal to form a slurry, the iron filings can easily be extracted with a magnet. You will see a noticeable accumulation of iron filings on the magnet after a few minutes of stirring.

Unfortunately, most of the elemental iron added to cereal cannot be absorbed by the body. The body can only use iron that has lost 2 electrons, causing the iron to have a charge of 2+. This iron is known as iron(II) or the ferrous form of iron. Many iron supplements contain this form of iron in the compound ferrous sulfate. The ferrous form of iron is readily absorbed by the body.

Your stomach acid will convert elemental iron to ferrous iron, but most of the iron will pass from your stomach before the acid can really do much. Cereal manufacturers could add this ferrous form of iron to cereal, but it would shorten the cereal's shelf life. Elemental iron never goes bad, but it may rust!

Experiment # 13:
ERASING A CASSETTE TAPE

Objective: To discover how cassette tapes work.

Materials:

- Old cassette tape

Safety Precautions: *Do not perform this experiment on a cassette tape you want to listen to again, as the Mega-Magnet will permanently destroy the tape!* Only use the Mega-Magnet under adult supervision. Keep the Mega-Magnet away from televisions, computers, software, videotapes, and credit cards.

Procedure:
1. Place the Mega-Magnet on the exposed portion of the tape and then advance the tape manually with a pencil or your finger.
2. Rewind the tape and listen to this portion. What do you observe?

Explanation: The part of the tape exposed to the Mega-Magnet will be permanently erased. That is why you do not want to place your Mega-Magnet near any type of cassette you want to keep.

The cassette tape is coated with tiny particles of ferric oxide, or Fe_2O_3. Another name for ferric oxide is iron(III) oxide.

During recording, these tiny particles are magnetically arranged in such a way as to produce specific sounds when played back. When a tape is erased by the machine, a magnet is drawn across the tape, removing the pattern of the tiny particles and thus the sound it could potentially create. For further evidence of the magnetic nature of these tapes, unravel it and then see if your Mega-Magnet is attracted to it.

Ferric oxide belongs to a class of compounds known as ferrites, which are termed ferrimagnetic. Ferrimagnetic substances are strongly attracted to a magnet, but their attraction is not as strong as that of a ferromagnetic substance. A compound of iron will usually not be as strongly attracted to a magnet as iron itself.

39 Amazing Experiments with the Mega-Magnet

Experiment # 14:
MAGNETIC FLOPPY DISKS

Objective: To determine how a floppy disk stores information.

Materials:

- Floppy disk

Safety Precautions: *Do not attempt this experiment on a floppy disk that you plan on reusing. This experiment will destroy the disk.* Only use the Mega-Magnet under adult supervision. Keep the Mega-Magnet away from televisions, computers, software, videotapes, cassette tapes, and credit cards.

Procedure:
1. Take apart a floppy disk that you no longer want.
2. Attempt to pick up the circular disk with the Mega-Magnet. Are you successful?
3. Turn the disk over. Is the Mega-Magnet attracted to both sides of the disk?

Explanation: The large black piece of flimsy plastic within a floppy disk stores information magnetically, due to a very thin coating of ferric oxide (Fe_2O_3) particles on the surface of both sides of the film. Since these particles are ferrimagnetic, the disk will be attracted to the Mega-Magnet. The Mega-Magnet will rearrange the tiny bits of magnetic material, permanently erasing anything stored there. It is therefore not a good idea to bring the Mega-Magnet anywhere near a floppy disk or hard drive that you want to keep from being erased.

Similar technology is used to encode information on credit cards and hotel room "keys." The Mega-Magnet can rearrange this magnetically recorded information and render them useless.

39 Amazing Experiments with the Mega-Magnet

CDs, on the other hand, do not store information magnetically. Tiny pits are "burned" into the surface of the disk, which can only be read by a laser. Even though the surface of your CD appears smooth, it is actually full of hills and valleys.

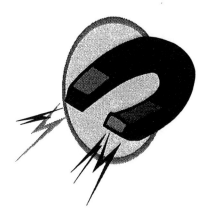

Experiment # 15:
IS YOUR SOIL MAGNETIC?

Objective: To discover if soil contains particles that are attracted to the Mega-Magnet.

Materials:
- Soil
- Cup

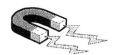

Safety Precautions: Only use the Mega-Magnet under adult supervision. Keep the Mega-Magnet away from televisions, computers, software, videotapes, cassette tapes, and credit cards.

Procedure:
1. Collect about a half-cup of soil (not dirt!) from your yard and place it into a disposable plastic cup or jar.
2. Pour enough water over this soil to completely cover it.
3. Now swirl your Mega-Magnet around in this soil-water suspension for several minutes. Many particles will be attracted to the magnet!

4. Remove these particles from the magnet and hold them a short distance away. What happens?

Explanation: The particles attracted to the Mega-Magnet are most likely composed of ferrites. Ferrites are a broad class of iron compounds containing iron, oxygen, and often another type of metal. An example of a ferrite is magnetite, which has the formula Fe_3O_4. Magnetite is ferrimagnetic, since it is not as strongly attracted to a magnet as is pure iron. The particles adhering to your magnet are most likely ferrimagnetic as well.

Iron is the fourth most abundant element in the earth's crust (after oxygen, silicon, and aluminum), making up about 5% of the earth's crust by mass. In the southern states, the soil is very red due to the abundance of iron oxides in the soil. Are these iron compounds attracted to a magnet? The next time you see some red clay, collect a sample and try it!

Experiment # 16:
DISTORTION OF A TV IMAGE

Objective: To discover the effect of a magnetic field on electrons.

Materials:

- Old television set

Safety Precautions: *Perform this experiment only on an old television set. This experiment may cause permanent damage to the television set!* Only use the Mega-Magnet under adult supervision. Keep the Mega-Magnet away from computers, software, videotapes, cassette tapes, and credit cards.

Procedure:
1. Turn on the television and place the Mega-Magnet on the screen.
2. Move the magnet rapidly over the screen and observe the effect.
3. Turn the magnet over and observe the direction in which the picture is deflected.

Explanation: The image on the television screen will be visibly distorted in the direction of the magnet. The picture tube in a television set is actually a cathode ray tube, which shoots beams of electrons towards the screen. These electrons illuminate the phosphor coating on the inside of the screen, creating a picture.

Electrons are deflected by a magnetic field, thus the image is distorted when a magnet is brought near. Depending on how the poles of the magnet are oriented, the picture on the screen will appear to be either deflected or attracted to the magnet. Really wild effects can be created using a color TV, but please remember that the long term effects on the television set are probably not good!

39 Amazing Experiments with the Mega-Magnet

Experiment # 17:
DEFLECTION OF ELECTRONS BY A MAGNETIC FIELD

Objective: To demonstrate the effect of a magnetic field on electrons.

Materials:
- Balloon
- Table salt

Safety Precautions: Only use the Mega-Magnet under adult supervision. Keep the Mega-Magnet away from televisions, computers, software, videotapes, cassette tapes, and credit cards.

Procedure:
1. Blow up a balloon and tie it off.
2. Sprinkle some table salt on a table.
3. Rub the balloon in your hair or on a wool sweater.
4. Bring the charged part of the balloon near the salt. Salt granules should readily fly up to adhere to the balloon. If not, try rubbing the balloon against a different

substance until enough static charge builds up to attract the salt.

5. Now, turn the balloon over so the salt particles which adhere to it are on top of the balloon.

6. Bring the Mega-Magnet very close to these salt particles on the balloon. What do you observe?

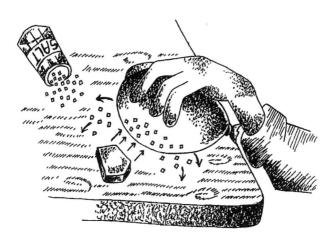

Explanation: When the balloon is rubbed in the hair, excess electrons from your hair are transferred to the balloon. These excess electrons are often referred to as static electricity. Since the balloon has an excess of electrons, the balloon is now negatively charged. Salt is composed of particles of sodium chloride. Sodium chloride is an ionic compound, being composed of positive ions of sodium and negative ions of chlorine. The positive charges in the salt are attracted to the negative charges on the balloon. It is the attraction of opposite charges that causes the salt granules to adhere to the balloon. When the Mega-Magnet is brought near the balloon, the excess electrons on the surface of the balloon are deflected. As a result, the salt particles no longer adhere to the balloon and they subsequently fly off. The deflection of electrons by a magnetic field was also responsible for the distortion of a TV picture in the previous experiment.

39 Amazing Experiments with the Mega-Magnet

Experiment # 18:
HOW DOES A COMPASS WORK?

Objective: To discover why a compass always points North.

Materials:

- Inexpensive compass

Safety Precautions: *Only use an inexpensive compass for this experiment. The compass may be permanently damaged by this experiment.* Only use the Mega-Magnet under adult supervision. Keep the Mega-Magnet away from televisions, computers, software, videotapes, cassette tapes, and credit cards.

Procedure:

1. Place the Mega-Magnet near the compass and watch the compass needle. What happens?
2. Move the Mega-Magnet in a circular motion and watch the compass hand.
3. Change the orientation of the Mega-Magnet and observe the effect it has on the compass needle.

39 Amazing Experiments with the Mega-Magnet

4. Attempt to determine how far away the Mega-Magnet can be from the compass and still be attracted to it.

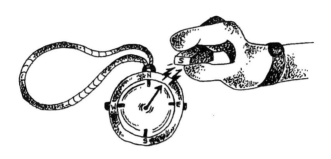

Explanation: The magnetic lines of force that arise from your compass needle line up parallel with the magnetic lines of force that extend from the poles of the earth. As a result, a compass points North, but not to the North Pole we see on a map. Instead, a compass points to what is called the magnetic *south* pole, about 1500 km from the geographic *north* pole. The magnetic south pole is just west of Baffin Island, Canada.

The needle of a compass is itself a magnet – with north and south poles. Since opposites attract, the north pole of a compass actually points to the magnetic south pole of the earth. The earth is actually a giant magnet, with poles on each end. The other end of a compass needle (the south pole of the compass) is attracted to the magnetic north pole, which is about 1500 km from the geographic south pole.

(To reduce confusion, some books refer to the magnetic pole nearest the geographic north pole as the magnetic north pole. However, since opposites attract, the north pole of a compass needle must then be referred to as the north-seeking pole. The important thing to remember is that opposite poles attract. There is nothing inherently north or south about either poles or compasses, only a need to recognize that the terms can be confused because a needle's north pole is attracted to a south pole on the earth, and vice versa.)

The needle of the compass will be attracted to the Mega-Magnet. Since the Mega-Magnet is so much closer to the compass than either magnetic pole, it attracts the compass needle, which is made of ferromagnetic material. As the magnet is moved, the compass needle will change direction. Remember that opposites attract, so the north pole of your compass will be attracted to the south pole of the Mega-Magnet. If a compass was placed directly on the North Pole, it would spin in circles!

When navigating with a map and compass, it is extremely important to remember that your compass needle points to the magnetic poles, not the geographic poles. If you do not realize this, you could end up getting seriously lost! In the contiguous United States, magnetic north can differ from geographic north by anywhere from

0° to 21°, and even more in Alaska and Canada. Maps which define the amount of the difference help users make necessary corrections. The angular difference between magnetic north and true north is known as declination on terrestrial maps. On nautical charts, the difference is known as variation.

Experiment # 19:
MAKE YOUR OWN MAGNET

Objective: To use one magnet to create another.

Materials:
- Iron nail
- Paper clips
- Hammer

Safety Precautions: Only use the Mega-Magnet under adult supervision. Keep the Mega-Magnet away from televisions, computers, software, videotapes, cassette tapes, and credit cards.

Procedure:
1. Stroke an iron nail in the same direction about 30 times with the Mega-Magnet.
2. Now attempt to use this nail to pick up a paper clip. Are you successful?
3. Now pound the side of the nail with a hammer several times. Attempt to pick up the paper clip with the nail. Are you successful now?

39 Amazing Experiments with the Mega-Magnet

FIRST

Explanation: By stroking the nail with the paper clip, tiny regions within the nail known as domains line up in the same direction. Within each domain are many electrons spinning in the same direction, generating a magnetic field. When these domains line up in the same direction, the combined magnetic field of these domains forms a magnet strong enough to pick up a paper clip.

When the nail is struck with a hammer, these domains become unaligned, tending to cancel out each other's magnetic fields. As a result, the nail is no longer able to pick up the paper clip.

39 Amazing Experiments with the Mega-Magnet

Experiment # 20:
SUSPENDING A PAPER CLIP

Objective: To construct an optical illusion that appears to defy gravity.

Materials:
- Pringle's potato chip can
- Pencil
- Thread
- Paper clip
- Scissors

Safety Precautions: Only use the
Mega-Magnet under adult supervision. Keep the Mega-Magnet away from televisions, computers, software, videotapes, cassette tapes, and credit cards.

Procedure:
1. Starting from the top of a Pringles potato chip can, cut a piece out from the side about 8 inches long by 3 inches wide. Do not cut all the way to the bottom of the can.
2. Turn the can upside down and place the Mega-Magnet inside the metal top of the

can. When viewed from the side, the Mega-Magnet should not be visible.

3. Now poke a sharp pencil through both sides of the can, toward the bottom of the open end.

4. Tie about a foot long piece of thread to the pencil, and tie the other end of the thread to a paper clip.

5. Now wind up the thread on the pencil until the paper clip is attracted by the magnet but does not touch it. The paper clip will now appear to be suspended in mid-air. Friends and family will be amazed!

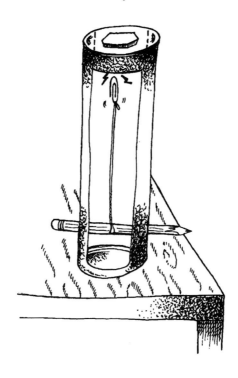

39 Amazing Experiments with the Mega-Magnet

Explanation: This is a fun experiment that can set up as a permanent display. The suspended paper clip will appear to defy gravity. Some forces can act at a distance, such as the force exerted by a magnet. Other forces that act at a distance are gravity and electrostatic forces (such as picking up bits of paper with a charged balloon). Some forces must be in contact to act, such as friction and buoyant force. Buoyant forces enable objects to float in a fluid.

39 Amazing Experiments with the Mega-Magnet

Experiment # 21:
MAKE YOUR OWN COMPASS

Objective: To make a compass.

Materials:

- Bathtub
- Large cork
- Paper clip
- Tape

Safety Precautions: Only use the Mega-Magnet under adult supervision. Keep the Mega-Magnet away from televisions, computers, software, videotapes, cassette tapes, and credit cards.

Procedure:
1. Straighten out a paper clip.
2. Tape it to the top of a large cork.
3. Stroke one end of the paper clip about 30 times in the same direction with the Mega-Magnet.
4. Float the cork in a bathtub or sink containing a few inches of water.
5. Bring the same side of the Mega-Magnet to the end of the paper clip that was stroked.

39 Amazing Experiments with the Mega-Magnet

6. Now bring the opposite end of the Mega-Magnet to the paper clip.
7. Repeat steps 5 and 6 with the other end of the paper clip.
8. Attempt to move your homemade compass around the bathtub with the Mega-Magnet.

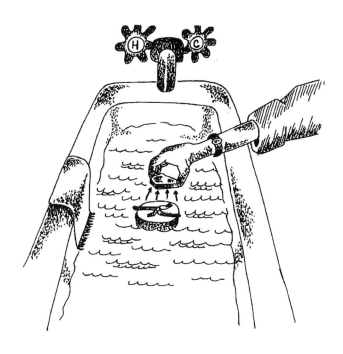

Explanation: Stroking the paper clip with the magnet will cause it to become magnetized. This occurs because the domains within the paper clip become aligned in the same direction. A

39 Amazing Experiments with the Mega-Magnet

domain is a region within an atom where many electrons spin in the same direction, giving rise to a magnetic field. When these domains all line up in the same direction, a magnet is formed.

Since the paper clip itself becomes a magnet, it too has a north and a south pole. Because like poles repel and opposite poles attract, the north pole of the paper clip magnet will be repelled by the north pole of the Mega-Magnet. The magnetized paper clip can act as a compass because its north pole is attracted to the magnetic south pole of the Earth.

39 Amazing Experiments with the Mega-Magnet

Experiment # 22:
EERIE EFFECTS

Objective: To demonstrate the ability of the Mega-Magnet to move objects without touching them.

Materials:

- Ferromagnetic objects (nuts, bolts, silverware, paper clips, etc.)
- Table

Safety Precautions: Only use the Mega-Magnet under adult supervision. Keep the Mega-Magnet away from televisions, computers, software, videotapes, cassette tapes, and credit cards.

Procedure:

1. Place several objects that you know to be attracted to a magnet on a tabletop.
2. Place the Mega-Magnet underneath the table and attempt to move these objects.

Explanation: Tell your friends that you can move these objects by thinking. Act as if you are concentrating, then make the objects move about the table. For best effect, you will have to disguise the movement of your hand under the

table. Many other eerie effects may be produced at the dinner table. Silverware can suddenly be made to move freely about. You may end up convincing some that you have a ghost before they realize the trick! Your friends may be momentarily amazed but explain to them that the feat is only a trick, due to the extremely strong magnetic field surrounding a Mega-Magnet, whose magnetic field has the ability to penetrate objects to a much greater extent than a typical magnet.

Experiment # 23:
KILLING TIME

Objective: To stop a watch or a clock.

Materials:

- Watch or clock with a metal hand

Safety Precautions: *Only perform this experiment on an inexpensive clock or watch – it may cause permanent damage to the timepiece!* Only use the Mega-Magnet under adult supervision. Keep the Mega-Magnet away from televisions, computers, software, videotapes, cassette tapes, and credit cards.

Procedure:

1. Place the Mega-Magnet directly on top of the second hand on a watch or clock. Observe.
2. Remove the Mega-Magnet. What happens?

Explanation: Is the Mega-Magnet strong enough to actually stop time? Not quite. But it is powerful enough to prevent the hands on a watch or clock from moving. This only works if the hands are made from a ferromagnetic material, from which most watch hands are constructed.

39 Amazing Experiments with the Mega-Magnet

Does the Mega-Magnet have an effect on a digital watch? Try it and find out!

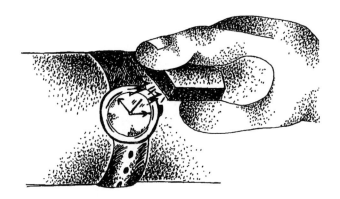

Experiment # 24:
FINDING THE POLES
OF THE MEGA-MAGNET

Objective: To locate the poles on the Mega-Magnet.

Materials:
- Piece of string
- Less powerful magnet

Safety Precautions: Only use the Mega-Magnet under adult supervision. Keep the Mega-Magnet away from televisions, computers, software, videotapes, cassette tapes, and credit cards.

Procedure:
1. Obtain a less powerful magnet and position it near the Mega-Magnet so you feel a repulsive force. Once you feel this repulsion, you have identified one of the poles of the Mega-Magnet.
2. Now try to find the other pole. It should be on the opposite side of the Mega-Magnet.
3. To determine the identity of each pole, tie a string around the *edge* of the Mega-Magnet and suspend it until it comes to a

complete stop. (This works best if the string is suspended from a stationary point on the ceiling.) The north pole of the Mega-Magnet will be pointing to the magnetic south pole (near the geographic north pole).

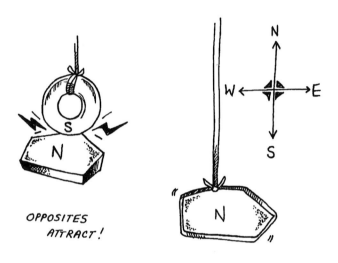

OPPOSITES ATTRACT!

Explanation: The repulsion you observed in this experiment is due to the fact that like poles repel one another, so if the south pole of a magnet is brought near the south pole of the Mega-Magnet, they will repel. The north pole of another magnet will be attracted to the south pole of the Mega-Magnet. Opposite poles attract. When suspended from a string, the north pole of the Mega-Magnet

39 Amazing Experiments with the Mega-Magnet

will point North. (As you may recall from earlier experiments, the north pole of a magnet actually points to the magnetic south pole, which is near the geographic north pole.) In this way, any magnet acts like a compass – they always point North!

Experiment # 25:
REPULSION OF LIKE POLES

Objective: To test the strength of the Mega-Magnet by measuring its repulsive force on a less powerful magnet.

Materials:
- Three doughnut-shaped magnets (available from a hardware store or Radio Shack)
- Two pencils

Safety Precautions: Only use the Mega-Magnet under adult supervision. Keep the Mega-Magnet away from televisions, computers, software, videotapes, cassette tapes, and credit cards.

Procedure:
1. Place the end of a pencil directly on top of the Mega-Magnet and then place a doughnut-shaped magnet through the pencil. If like poles are facing one another, the magnets will be repelled. Measure how high the magnet is suspended.
2. Now suspend one of the doughnut-shaped magnets above another similar magnet,

39 Amazing Experiments with the Mega-Magnet

and measure how high it is suspended. How does the height of suspension compare with the magnet suspended over the Mega-Magnet?

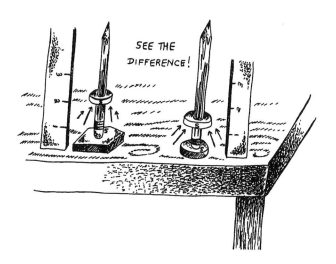

SEE THE DIFFERENCE!

Explanation: You should observe that the doughnut-shaped magnet is suspended much higher over the Mega-Magnet than over an ordinary magnet. Just as the Mega-Magnet has a much greater attractive force than most magnets, it likewise has a much greater repulsive force. Since like poles repel, this experiment only works if similar poles of each magnet are facing one another.

39 Amazing Experiments with the Mega-Magnet

Magnetic repulsion has exceptional potential for a variety of applications. Several countries are developing magnetically levitated trains (abbreviated as maglev) that operate on the principle of repulsion of like poles. If the bottom of the train has the same magnetic polarity as the train tracks, then the train will be "levitated." The train actually never touches the track at all, but "floats" about 10 mm above the surface, so there is no friction between the train and the track—although the train still must overcome air resistance. Since no moving parts are involved, little maintenance is required. The trains are also very quiet, and can attain speeds of up to 500 km/hr (300 mi/hr). The maglev trains are accelerated by changing magnetic fields in the track.

Experiment # 26:
DO ELECTRIC CURRENTS PRODUCE MAGNETIC FIELDS?

Objective: To demonstrate the relationship between magnetism and electricity.

Materials:
- Battery
- One foot length of copper wire

Safety Precautions: Only use the Mega-Magnet under adult supervision. Keep the Mega-Magnet away from televisions, computers, software, videotapes, cassette tapes, and credit cards.

Procedure:
1. Strip the insulation away from both ends of a copper wire. Fold the wire into a "U" shape.
2. Place the exposed ends of the wire on opposite terminals of the battery.
3. While holding the wire on the battery terminals, bring the closed end of the loop toward the end of the Mega-Magnet. What happens?

39 Amazing Experiments with the Mega-Magnet

4. Turn the Mega-Magnet around so the opposite side is facing the loop. What happens now?

Explanation: When the wire is connected to the battery, it conducts a current. This current produces a magnetic field, which is either repelled or attracted to the Mega-Magnet, depending on its orientation. You will notice that the wire moves the greatest distance when placed on the end of the Mega-Magnet. Why is this, when the poles are oriented on opposite faces of the Mega-Magnet?

The magnetic field lines of the Mega-Magnet will line up at a point perpendicular to the current carrying wire. Therefore the force of attraction (or repulsion) will be the greatest when the current flow within the wire is perpendicular to the direction of the magnetic field. This occurs on the ends of the magnet, not the faces where the poles are located. If the wire was placed on the face of the magnet, then the magnetic field lines would be parallel to the electric current in the wire. On the ends of the magnet, the wire is perpendicular to the magnetic field.

This experiment was first performed in 1820 by Hans Christian Oersted, a Dutch physicist and chemist. He was seeking to find a connection between magnetism and electricity. This experiment revealed that an electric current produces a magnetic field.

A similar effect can be created by coiling a wire around a nail, and then connecting both ends of the wire to a battery. The nail then becomes magnetized, and it can pick up ferromagnetic objects such as paper clips. The nail itself becomes an electromagnet, since electricity is producing a magnetic field. The greater the number of coils of wire that are present, the stronger the magnetic field.

Experiment # 27:
DEMONSTRATION OF EDDY CURRENTS

Objective: To observe the effect of eddy currents in a copper pipe.

Materials:
- Hollow copper pipe approximately 6 feet long, with a 1 inch diameter
- Quarter or other piece of metal that is not attracted to a magnet
- Stopwatch

Safety Precautions: Only use the Mega-Magnet under adult supervision. Keep the Mega-Magnet away from televisions, computers, software, videotapes, cassette tapes, and credit cards.

Procedure:
1. Hold the copper pipe completely vertical, and drop the quarter down the pipe.
2. Record the time it takes the quarter to fall through the pipe.
3. Now drop the Mega-Magnet down the pipe.
4. Record how long it takes for the Mega-Magnet to fall through the pipe.

39 Amazing Experiments with the Mega-Magnet

5. Repeat the experiment, except now hold the pipe at an angle. What happens to the Mega-Magnet's rate of fall?

Explanation: Since copper is not attracted to a magnet, why does it take so long for the magnet to travel through the pipe? A very interesting phenomenon is at work. As the magnet moves through the pipe, it creates an electrical current in the metal, known as an eddy current. As the name implies, eddy currents move in a swirling or circular fashion. Any moving magnetic field will create an electrical current. These currents in turn create a magnetic field, which repels the magnetic field of the magnet as it moves down the pipe. This slows the magnet down. The magnet still falls, due to gravity, since the magnetic field generated by the eddy currents is not strong enough to stop the magnet completely. Another way to feel the effects of the eddy currents is to rub the magnet along the outside of the copper pipe.

Eddy currents can be produced in other metals besides copper. Try dropping the Mega-Magnet through a tube of aluminum foil. What happens? If the Mega-Magnet is rubbed along the outside of the roll of foil, can you feel the repulsive force? Yet another way to demonstrate eddy currents is to slide the Mega-Magnet down an inclined plane of any type of sheet metal (as long as the metal is not ferromagnetic). The formation of eddy currents will very noticeably slow the rate of fall of the Mega-Magnet as it slides down an inclined plane.

There are many practical situations where eddy currents have been put to use. From this experiment, you can see that eddy currents have the ability to slow down certain objects. This effect has been put to use in the braking systems of rapid-transit rail cars. Induced eddy currents from an electromagnet can cause a repulsive force to be exerted either on a metal wheel or the rail itself. Eddy currents decrease as the car slows down, which allows the car to brake smoothly.

When a coin is inserted in an American vending machine, it falls between the poles of a magnet. Eddy currents are produced in the coin as it falls through the magnetic field. These induced eddy currents slow the coin down. Since every metallic alloy will be slowed down at a different rate, counterfeit coins can be detected.

Experiment # 28:
DEMONSTRATION OF EDDY CURRENTS: PART 2

Objective: To demonstrate the effect of eddy currents in aluminum.

Materials:
- Japanese yen or other aluminum coin (available in a coin shop)
- Electric drill

Safety Precautions: Only use the Mega-Magnet under adult supervision. Keep the Mega-Magnet away from televisions, computers, software, videotapes, cassette tapes, and credit cards. Use an electric drill only under adult supervision.

Procedure:
1. Test the yen with the Mega-Magnet to verify that it is not ferromagnetic.
2. Place the yen on its edge on a flat table.
3. Swiftly move the Mega-Magnet back and forth directly above and very close to the yen. Be careful not to touch the coin with

the Mega-Magnet. Observe. It may take a little practice to perfect this technique.

4. Now place the yen flat on the table. Quickly place the Mega-Magnet on top of the yen and then just as quickly remove the Mega-Magnet. You should be able to lift the yen completely off the table.

5. Place the Mega-Magnet on the end of an electric drill and bring it close to a yen that is lying flat on the table. Turn on the drill. What happens to the yen? Reverse the direction of the drill. What happens?

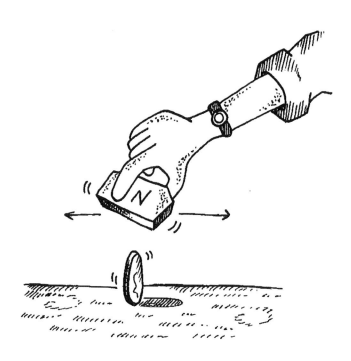

39 Amazing Experiments with the Mega-Magnet

Explanation: The yen will move back and forth very rapidly, almost as if it is being moved by remote control. This is especially interesting because the yen, being made of aluminum, is not attracted to a magnet. Eddy currents are being produced in the aluminum by the rapidly moving magnetic field surrounding the Mega-Magnet. These eddy currents in turn generate a magnetic field in the yen, which is repelled by the magnetic field of the Mega-Magnet. As a result of this repulsion, the yen moves. For the same reason, the yen can be momentarily lifted off the table. The strongest eddy currents are produced when the Mega-Magnet is attached to a drill. This causes the yen to move very rapidly.

39 Amazing Experiments with the Mega-Magnet

Experiment # 29:
IS WATER MAGNETIC?

Objective: To demonstrate the diamagnetism of water.

Materials:

- 70% Isopropyl rubbing alcohol
- Olive oil
- Medicine dropper
- Transparent plastic cup

Safety Precautions: Isopropyl alcohol is poisonous if ingested and is flammable. Exercise caution. Only use the Mega-Magnet under adult supervision. Keep the Mega-Magnet away from televisions, computers, software, videotapes, cassette tapes, and credit cards.

Procedure:

1. Fill a transparent disposable plastic cup about halfway with 70% isopropyl rubbing alcohol.
2. Using a medicine dropper, add several dropperfuls of olive oil. The olive oil, since it is insoluble in alcohol, should form into many separate spheres. Since it is denser than alcohol, it should concentrate on the bottom.

39 Amazing Experiments with the Mega-Magnet

3. Now add water drop by drop until some of the balls of olive oil become suspended in the middle of the water-alcohol solution. They are now in a state of neutral buoyancy, having the same density as the solution, neither sinking nor floating.
4. Now submerge the Mega-Magnet in the solution, bringing it very close to a drop of olive oil. What do you observe?

39 Amazing Experiments with the Mega-Magnet

Explanation: The olive oil will appear to jump toward the magnet. This does not mean that the oil is attracted to the magnet, however. The water in the alcohol solution (70% isopropyl alcohol contains 30% water) is actually repulsed by the magnet, which gives the appearance of the oil being attracted to the magnet. Since water is diamagnetic, it is slightly repelled by a magnetic force.

Diamagnetism is a much weaker force than ferromagnetism, which is why the force of repulsion observed in this experiment will be slight. Any object with a high water content will be diamagnetic as well. This includes fruits, frogs, and people. Frogs have actually been levitated using very powerful electromagnets, with no harm done to the frog!

39 Amazing Experiments with the Mega-Magnet

Experiment # 30:
IS WATER MAGNETIC?
PART 2

Objective: To demonstrate the diamagnetism of water.

Materials:
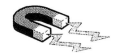
- Drinking straw
- Two grapes
- Thread

Safety Precautions: Only use the Mega-Magnet under adult supervision. Keep the Mega-Magnet away from televisions, computers, software, videotapes, cassette tapes, and credit cards.

Procedure:
1. Tie a piece of thread about 2 feet long around the center of a drinking straw.
2. Suspend the straw from the edge of a table so it hangs freely.
3. Place a grape on each end of the straw by poking the straw through each grape.
4. Adjust the thread so that the straw and grapes balance horizontally.
5. Bring the Mega-Magnet slowly toward one of the grapes. What happens?

39 Amazing Experiments with the Mega-Magnet

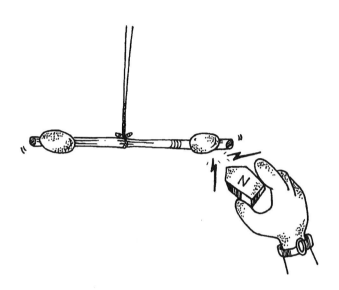

Explanation: The grape will be repelled by the Mega-Magnet. As we saw in the previous experiment, water is diamagnetic, which means it is slightly repelled by a magnetic field. Since grapes are over 80% water by mass, they will be repelled by a magnetic field.

39 Amazing Experiments with the Mega-Magnet

Experiment # 31:
ARE IRON TABLETS ATTRACTED TO A MAGNET?

Objective: To discover if the Mega-Magnet will be attracted to the iron in a compound.

Materials:
- Ferrous sulfate tablets (available from a drug store)
- Scotch tape

Safety Precautions: Ferrous sulfate tablets are especially toxic to young children. Store out of the reach of children. Only use the Mega-Magnet under adult supervision. Keep the Mega-Magnet away from televisions, computers, software, videotapes, cassette tapes, and credit cards.

Procedure:
1. Tape a ferrous sulfate tablet to the bottom of a piece of scotch tape about 6 inches long, allowing it to dangle freely.
2. Hold the tape from the top and bring the Mega-Magnet near the iron tablet. What happens?

39 Amazing Experiments with the Mega-Magnet

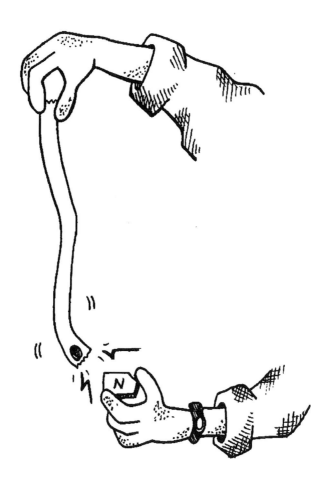

Explanation: Iron supplements are often sold in the form of ferrous sulfate. The ferrous form of iron has a charge of 2+, and is often referred to as Iron(II). This form of iron is readily available to the body. The tablet is attracted to the Mega-Magnet, due to the fact that it contains

39 Amazing Experiments with the Mega-Magnet

iron, which is a ferromagnetic element. However, it should be evident that the attraction of the Mega-Magnet for the iron tablet is much less than the attraction for iron alone. When iron reacts with another element to form a compound, its electron structure completely changes. In an ionic compound, for example, some electrons are transferred from the iron to the sulfate group. The 2+ form of iron has lost 2 electrons. As a result, some compounds of iron will be paramagnetic, which means they are only slightly attracted to a magnet. Other paramagnetic substances include aluminum, tin, platinum, and tungsten.

Experiment # 32:
PARAMAGNETISM OF OXYGEN

Objective: To discover if oxygen is attracted to a magnet.

Materials:

- 3% hydrogen peroxide
- Active, dry yeast
- Petri dish, or other shallow dish

Safety Precautions: Hydrogen peroxide is toxic if ingested. Store out of reach of children. Only use the Mega-Magnet under adult supervision. Keep the Mega-Magnet away from televisions, computers, software, videotapes, cassette tapes, and credit cards.

Procedure:

1. Add enough hydrogen peroxide to cover the bottom of the dish.
2. Add a quarter-teaspoon of yeast.
3. When bubbles form, place the Mega-Magnet magnet in the dish.
4. Slide the Mega-Magnet toward the bubbles. What happens?

39 Amazing Experiments with the Mega-Magnet

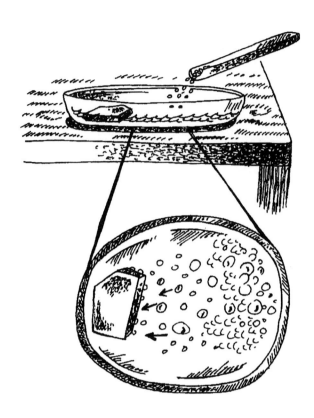

Explanation: The yeast acts as a catalyst, breaking down the hydrogen peroxide into water and oxygen. The bubbles that form are bubbles of oxygen. These bubbles will be attracted to the Mega-Magnet. Oxygen is a paramagnetic substance, which means it is slightly attracted to a magnet. If you ever have access to liquid oxygen, droplets of it are readily attracted to the Mega-Magnet.

39 Amazing Experiments with the Mega-Magnet

Experiment # 33:
MAGNETIZING A HAMMER

Objective: To transform a hammer into a magnet.

Materials:

- Claw hammer (head must be made from steel)
- Paper clips
- Inexpensive compass

Safety Precautions: Only use the Mega-Magnet under adult supervision. Keep the Mega-Magnet away from televisions, computers, software, videotapes, cassette tapes, and credit cards. Only use an inexpensive compass for this experiment, as it may cause permanent damage to the compass.

Procedure:

1. Place the Mega-Magnet on the end of the head of the hammer.
2. Now place two paper clips, one on each "claw" of the hammer. They should be attracted to it.
3. Gently move one of the paper clips toward

the other. What happens?
4. Bring a compass near each paper clip. What do you observe?
5. Remove the Mega-Magnet from the hammer head and bring the same side of the magnet that was against the hammer near the compass. What do you observe?
6. Observe the paper clips that were attached to the hammer. Do they remain attached?
7. Now place the other side of the Mega-Magnet on the head of the hammer. What immediately happens to the paper clips?
8. Place the paper clips on the claw of the hammer again. Now bring each near a compass. What do you observe?
9. Remove the Mega-Magnet and bring the same side of the magnet that was against the hammer near the compass. What do you observe?

Explanation: If the head of the hammer is made of steel, the Mega-Magnet will be attracted to it. The paper clips will be attracted to the hammer, since the hammer itself becomes a temporary magnet when it comes into contact with the Mega-Magnet. When you attempt to move the paper clips together, you will notice a definite repulsion as one paper clip moves away from the other. This occurs because each paper clip also becomes temporarily magnetized, and when one pole of a temporary magnet is brought near the

39 Amazing Experiments with the Mega-Magnet

like pole of another temporary magnet, repulsion results.

When brought near a compass, each of the paper clips will attract the same pole of the compass, verifying that each paper clip becomes a magnet, with its poles oriented in the same direction. If the Mega-Magnet is removed, and the same side of the magnet that was attached to the hammer is brought near the compass, the compass needle will move in the same direction as it did when the paper clips were brought near it.

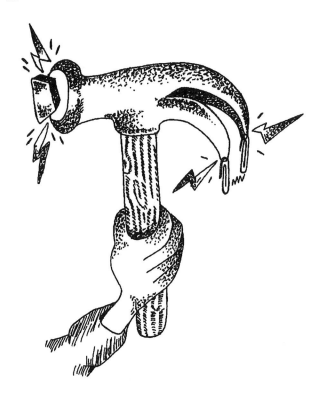

39 Amazing Experiments with the Mega-Magnet

The poles of the paper clip magnet will be oriented in the same direction as the poles of the Mega-Magnet, whereas the poles of the hammer head will be oriented differently. This is because opposite poles are attracted to one another, and like poles repel. For example, when the north pole of the Mega-Magnet sticks to the hammer, the hammer becomes a magnet, with the south pole of this magnet facing the north pole of the Mega-Magnet. Then the opposite side of the hammer head will become the north pole. The paper clip (which also becomes a magnet) will have its south pole toward the north pole of the hammer, and the paper clip's north pole will then attract the south pole of the compass.

You will notice that when the Mega-Magnet is removed from the head of the hammer, the paper clips remain attached. This is because the hammer head remains temporarily magnetized even after the Mega-Magnet is removed. But when the Mega-Magnet is reversed, and the opposite pole is placed on the head of the hammer, the paper clips are immediately repelled. If the north pole of the magnet now faces the hammer, then the opposite side of the hammer will become the south pole of the temporary hammer head magnet. Since the south pole of the paper clip magnets face the south pole of the hammer magnet, then the paper clips will be immediately repelled and fall off.

These paper clips can be easily reattached, however. But their poles will now be reversed. If the paper clips are brought near the compass now, they will attract the opposite pole of the compass as before. If the same pole of the Mega-Magnet that faced the hammer is brought near the compass, the compass will now point in the same direction as it did when the paper clips were brought near it.

39 Amazing Experiments with the Mega-Magnet

Experiment # 34:
OBSERVATION OF THE CURIE POINT

Objective: To discover the effect of temperature on a ferromagnetic substance.

Materials:
- Propane torch
- Tongs
- Safety goggles
- Canadian nickel minted before 1982
- Brick

Safety Precautions: Use a propane torch only under adult supervision. Do not touch the coin after it has been heated. Only use the Mega-Magnet under adult supervision. Keep the Mega-Magnet away from televisions, computers, software, videotapes, cassette tapes, and credit cards.

Procedure:
1. Test a Canadian nickel or other Canadian coin with the Mega-Magnet to make sure it is attracted.
2. Using a pair of tongs, heat the coin strongly in the flame of a propane torch for several minutes, until the coin is red hot.

3. Place the red-hot coin on a brick or other fireproof surface. Be careful not to touch the coin.
4. Hold the Mega-Magnet with a pair of tongs directly over, but not touching, the coin. *It is extremely important to hold the Mega-Magnet with a pair of tongs, so as to prevent the red-hot coin from accidentally coming into contact with your skin.*
5. At first, nothing will happen, but eventually the coin will fly up into the air to meet the Mega-Magnet.

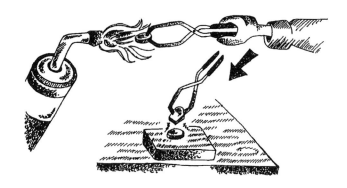

39 Amazing Experiments with the Mega-Magnet

Explanation: If you were to heat a magnet, it would lose its magnetic properties. Likewise, substances attracted to a magnet will also lose their magnetic properties if heated. The loss occurs because the domains—regions within a substance where all of the atoms point in the same direction—become random and unaligned. When these domains no longer are lined up, all magnetic properties are lost. The Curie point is the temperature at which a substance is no longer attracted to a magnet. For iron, this is 770°C; for nickel it is 358°C. Heating a ferromagnetic substance to a temperature above its Curie point will cause it lose its ferromagnetic properties. Once the substance cools to below its Curie temperature, its ferromagnetic properties return.

Canadian coins are magnetic because they are primarily made of nickel. After heating to a temperature above its Curie point (358°C), these coins will no longer be attracted to a magnet. However, once the coin cools to below its Curie point, its domains will once again become aligned, and it will suddenly fly up into the air to meet the Mega-Magnet! When finished, rinse the coin, tongs, and magnet with plenty of cold water to ensure that they are cool before you touch.

The Curie temperature is named after the French physicist Pierre Curie, who first discovered this phenomenon. At very low temperatures, several other elements and alloys become ferromagnetic. Since room temperature (25°C) is far above their Curie temperature, the ferromagnetism of these elements is not normally observed. The following chart lists the known ferromagnetic elements and their Curie temperature:

Element	Curie temperature (°C)
Cobalt	1120
Iron	770
Nickel	358
Gadolinium	19
Terbium	-52
Dysprosium	-188
Thulium	-251
Holmium	-253
Erbium	-253

39 Amazing Experiments with the Mega-Magnet

Experiment # 35:
A MAGNETIC MARBLE GAME

Objective: To observe the effect of the Mega-Magnet on a moving object.

Materials:
- Magnetic marbles (available from a toy store) or steel ball bearings (available from a hardware store)
- Thin board
- Duct tape

Safety Precautions: Only use the Mega-Magnet under adult supervision. Keep the Mega-Magnet away from televisions, computers, software, videotapes, cassette tapes, and credit cards.

Procedure:
1. Elevate one end of a thin board or heavy piece of cardboard with some books to form an inclined plane.
2. Tape the Mega-Magnet with duct tape under one end of the board, toward the bottom of the inclined plane, off to one side.
3. Roll the magnetic marbles or ball bearings

down the plane. What happens to them?

4. Incline the board at a greater angle. Can you make the magnetic marbles roll so fast that they are not stopped by the Mega-Magnet?

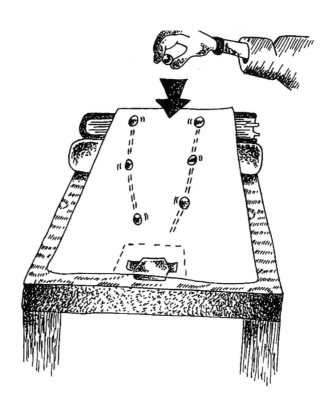

39 Amazing Experiments with the Mega-Magnet

Explanation: The magnetic marbles will be attracted to the Mega-Magnet, causing them to stop. Move the Mega-Magnet around to see how it affects the motion of the magnetic marbles. Turn the Mega-Magnet around to reverse the poles, and then see how this affects the motion of the magnetic marbles. Do not tell your friends that the Mega-Magnet is underneath the board, and then challenge them to come up with an explanation.

Experiment # 36:
STUD FINDER

Objective: To use the Mega-Magnet to detect the framing studs within your wall.

Materials:
- Wall containing wood studs

Safety Precautions: Only use the Mega-Magnet under adult supervision. Keep the Mega-Magnet away from televisions, computers, software, videotapes, cassette tapes, and credit cards.

Procedure:
1. Move the Mega-Magnet in a sweeping motion across a wall in your home, until the Mega-Magnet sticks to the wall.
2. Move the Mega-Magnet across the top of your countertop. Do you detect an attraction for a ferromagnetic object underneath?

Explanation: The many amazing uses for the Mega-Magnet are seemingly endless. Here is a very practical use for anyone who wants to find the studs in a wall, for purposes of hanging a picture or a clock. Eventually, the Mega-Magnet

39 Amazing Experiments with the Mega-Magnet

will encounter a nail head if swept across a wall, at which point the Mega-Magnet will stick to the wall! Wherever a nail is driven into the wall, there must be a stud. This works especially well on drywall; on other types of building materials results may vary.

Similar results are encountered when the Mega-Magnet is swept across the top of your kitchen countertop. Every few feet, you may feel a definite attraction to a bolt underneath the countertop, which is used to hold it in place.

39 Amazing Experiments with the Mega-Magnet

Experiment # 37:
A MAGNETIC PENDULUM

Objective: To observe the motion of a magnetic pendulum.

Materials:
- Pringle's potato chip can
- Pencil
- String
- Doughnut-shaped magnet (available from Radio Shack)

Safety Precautions: Only use the Mega-Magnet under adult supervision. Keep the Mega-Magnet away from televisions, computers, software, videotapes, cassette tapes, and credit cards.

Procedure:
1. Cut away the sides from a Pringle's potato chip can, except for a pair of one-inch wide strips on opposite ends of the can.
2. About a half-inch from the top, poke a small hole through each of these strips with a pair of scissors.
3. Insert a pencil through the hole in one strip and out the other hole in the other strip.

4. Tie a string to this pencil, and to the other end of the string tie a doughnut-shaped magnet. This will form your pendulum. The magnet should be about two inches from the metal base of the Pringle's can.

5. Now place the Mega-Magnet under the metal base and then swing the pendulum. You may need to adjust the length of the string for the optimal effect. What do you observe?

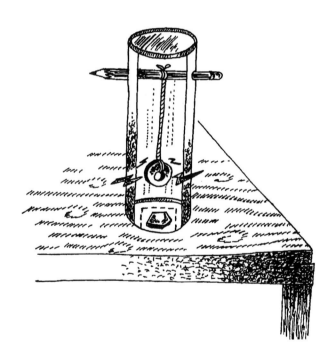

39 Amazing Experiments with the Mega-Magnet

Explanation: The pendulum will move in a very chaotic, random manner, encountering forces of attraction and repulsion as it passes over the Mega-Magnet. The magnetic pendulum is a good example of a chaotic system, because it is impossible to predict with certainty the exact path that the pendulum will take. Try varying the length of the string to achieve different effects. Turn your Mega-Magnet over to reverse the polarity. Do you see a difference in the movement of the pendulum?

An interesting variation on this pendulum involves swinging a magnet over a sheet of copper or aluminum. Eddy currents will be produced in the metal by the moving magnetic field, causing the magnet to noticeably slow down as it passes over the metal.

Why is the path of the magnetic pendulum, or any pendulum for that matter, impossible to predict? This is primarily due to the impossibility of making sure that the initial conditions of any two pendulum swings are identical. Even extremely minute initial changes in position or velocity will produce very significant changes in the ultimate path the pendulum takes. It appears that any chaotic system is extremely sensitive to initial conditions.

Chaos theory is becoming an increasingly important field of research. It has been used to study everything from measles outbreaks to heart rhythms to the stock market. Systems that were previously thought to be stable and predictable, like the movement of planets in our solar system, are now believed to have an element of unpredictability. Even the dripping of a water faucet is chaotic! By studying chaos, scientists hope to bring it under control. The only way to ultimately harness chaos is to seek to understand its causes.

Experiment # 38:
MAGNETIC PAINT

Objective: To discover how magnetic paint works.

Materials:
- Magnetic paint (available from some hardware stores or from Kling Magnetics, Inc., at www.kling.com or 518-392-4000)
- Small aluminum pie pan

Safety Precautions: *Do not place the Mega-Magnet in the paint. The paint will be very difficult to remove!* Only use the Mega-Magnet under adult supervision. Keep the Mega-Magnet away from televisions, computers, software, videotapes, cassette tapes, and credit cards.

Procedure:
1. Stir the magnetic paint thoroughly before using. Pour a small amount in a small aluminum pie pan, enough to cover the bottom of the pan.
2. Bring the Mega-Magnet to the underside of the pan. Observe the pattern that forms in the magnetic paint. Be careful not to allow the Mega-Magnet to come into contact with the paint.

39 Amazing Experiments with the Mega-Magnet

Explanation: Magnetic paint is normal acrylic latex paint to which has been added iron powder. The iron powder causes it to be ferromagnetic. When the Mega-Magnet is brought to the underside of the aluminum pie pan, the iron is drawn from the paint and attracted to the Mega-Magnet, forming an interesting spiked pattern that outlines the magnetic field of the Mega-Magnet. When a wall is painted with the magnetic paint, the Mega-Magnet will be readily attracted to it. The use of magnetic paint will turn any wall into a ferromagnetic surface that a magnet can be stuck to.

Another interesting magnetic fluid is termed ferrofluid, and is composed of ferrimagnetic magnetite that has been suspended in an oil-based

39 Amazing Experiments with the Mega-Magnet

substance. When a Mega-Magnet is brought near to the ferrofluid, it produces a fascinating spiked pattern that is similar to that of the magnetic paint. Ferrofluid was first developed by NASA in 1965 for the space program. A ferrofluid kit can be purchased from the Ferrofluidics Coroporation. They can be contacted at www.ferrofluidics.com or 603-883-9800.

39 Amazing Experiments with the Mega-Magnet

Experiment # 39:
STORING YOUR MEGA-MAGNET

Objective: To create an interesting optical illusion while storing your Mega-Magnet.

Materials:
- Cereal box
- Refrigerator

Safety Precautions: Do not place the Mega-Magnet directly on the refrigerator door, or the magnet may scratch the door when you attempt to remove it. Only use the Mega-Magnet under adult supervision. Keep the Mega-Magnet away from televisions, computers, software, videotapes, cassette tapes, and credit cards.

Procedure:
1. Place the Mega-Magnet inside of a box of cereal.
2. Place the box of cereal on the refrigerator door. Like magic, the cereal box stays suspended on the refrigerator door!

Explanation: Since it is so important to keep the Mega-Magnet away from computers, televisions, and the like, it is imperative that a

39 Amazing Experiments with the Mega-Magnet

suitable place be found to store the Mega-Magnet. The refrigerator door makes a great place. Your friends will be amazed when they see boxes of cereal suspended from the refrigerator door in apparent defiance of gravity. The Mega-Magnet also makes a great refrigerator magnet, enabling you to display all sorts of pictures or heavy items that a conventional magnet would not support. Even while your Mega-Magnet is resting, it is still performing amazing feats!

39 Amazing Experiments with the Mega-Magnet

LEARN MORE ABOUT MAGNETS

To learn more about magnets, check out the following web sites on the Internet:

Magnet Man: Cool Experiments with Magnets
http://my.execpc.com/~rhoadley/magindex.htm

The Exploratorium: Snacks About Magnetism
http://www.exploratorium.edu/snacks/ iconmagnetism.html

Magnets
http://www.uen.org/utahlink/lp_res/ TRB031.html

Magnet and Magnetism FAQ
http://www.wondermagnet.com/dev/ magfaq.html

Magnetism
http://www.hightechhigh.org/magnets/

Electricity and Magnetism
http://theory.uwinnipeg.ca/mod_tech/ node83.html

Magnet Experiments
http://education.wes.army.mil/clubhouse/ science/magnets.html

39 Amazing Experiments with the Mega-Magnet

BIBLIOGRAPHY

Beaty, Bill. "Neodymium Supermagnets: Some Demonstrations." http://amasci.com/ neodemo.html

Becker, Robert. "Mega-Magnet Chem Fax," Flinn Scientific, Inc. Batavia, Ill. 1993.

Dougherty, Paul and Cassidy, John. *Magnetic Magic.* Klutz: Palo Alto, CA, 1994.

Giancoli, Douglas C., *Physics: 2nd Edition.* Prentice Hall, Inc.: Englewood Cliffs, NJ, 1985.

Lee, E.W. *Magnetism, An Introductory Survey.* Dover Publications, Inc.: New York, NY, 1970.

Levine, Shar and Johnstone, Leslie. *The Magnet Book.* Sterling Publishing Company, Inc.: New York, NY, 1997.

Livingston, James D., *Driving Force: The Natural Magic of Magnets.* Harvard University Press: Cambridge, Mass. and London, England, 1996.

McCoy, Bob. *Quack! Tales of Medical Fraud from the Museum of Questionable Medical Devices.* Santa Monica Press: Santa Monica, CA, 2000.

39 Amazing Experiments with the Mega-Magnet

Rathjen, Don and Doherty, Paul. *Square Wheels and Other Easy-to-Build, Hands-On Science Activities.* Exploratorium Teacher Institute: San Francisco, CA, 2002.

Seidman, David. *The Essential Wilderness Navigator.* Ragged Mountain Press: Camden, Maine, 1995.

Vecchione, Glen. *Magnet Science.* Sterling Publishing Company, Inc.: New York, NY, 1995.

Wilson, Jerry and Buffa, Anthony. *Physics.* Prentice Hall, Inc.: Upper Saddle River, NJ, 2000.

NOTES:

39 *Amazing Experiments with the Mega-Magnet*

NOTES:_____

_____

_____

_____

_____

_____

_____

_____

_____

_____

_____

_____

_____

_____

39 Amazing Experiments with the Mega-Magnet

NOTES:

NOTES:_____

_____

_____

_____

_____

_____

_____

_____

_____

_____

_____

_____

_____

39 Amazing Experiments with the Mega-Magnet

NOTES:

_____

_____

_____

_____

_____

_____

_____

_____

_____

_____

_____

_____

39 Amazing Experiments with the Mega-Magnet

NOTES:

_____

_____

_____

_____

_____

_____

_____

_____

_____

_____

_____

_____

39 Amazing Experiments with the Mega-Magnet